D1368678

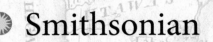
Smithsonian

Exploring
the
Maryland
Colony

by Robin S. Doak

CAPSTONE PRESS
a capstone imprint

Smithsonian books are published by Capstone Press,
1710 Roe Crest Drive, North Mankato, Minnesota 56003
www.capstonepub.com

Library of Congress Cataloging-in-Publication Data
Names: Doak, Robin S. (Robin Santos), 1963–author.
Title: Exploring the Maryland Colony/by Robin S. Doak.
Description: North Mankato, Minnesota: Capstone Press, [2017] |
   Series: Smithsonian. Exploring the 13 Colonies | Includes bibliographical
   references and index.
Identifiers: LCCN 2016005493
ISBN 9781515722380 (library binding)
ISBN 9781515722519 (paperback)
ISBN 9781515722649 (ebook PDF)
Subjects: LCSH: Maryland—History—Colonial period, ca. 1600–1775—Juvenile literature.
Maryland—History—1775–1865—Juvenile literature.
Classification: LCC F184 .D63 2017 | DDC 975.2/02—dc23
LC record available at http://lccn.loc.gov/2016005493

Editorial Credits
Jennifer Huston, editor; Richard Parker, designer; Eric Gohl, media researcher;
Kathy McColley, production specialist

Our very special thanks to Stephen Binns at the Smithsonian Center for Learning and Digital Access for
his curatorial review. Capstone would also like to thank Kealy Gordon, Smithsonian Institution Product
Development Manager, and the following at Smithsonian Enterprises: Christopher A. Liedel, President;
Carol LeBlanc, Senior Vice President; Brigid Ferraro, Vice President; Ellen Nanney, Licensing Manager.

Photo Credits
Bridgeman Images: Virginia Historical Society, Richmond, Virginia, USA, 23; Capstone: 4; Corbis: cover,
25, Lowell Georgia, 20 (left); CriaImages.com: Jay Robert Nash Collection, 11, 19, 38; Getty Images:
Hulton Archive, 22, 26, 27, Stock Montage, 36; Glow Images: SuperStock, 17; Granger, NYC: 9, 16, 28,
29, 31, 33, 35; iStockphoto: vicm, 20 (right); Maryland State Archives: 37; National Geographic Creative:
Louis Glanzman, 21; Newscom: Prisma/Album, 34 (right); North Wind Picture Archives: 5, 6, 13, 14,
15, 18, 24, 32, 39; Wikimedia: Public Domain, 12, 20 (middle), 30, 34 (left), 41

Design Elements: Shutterstock

Printed and bound in the USA.
009669F16

Table of Contents

Introduction:
The 13 Colonies

In the early 1600s, men, women, and children looking for a better life left Europe to establish **colonies** in North America. A colony is a settlement or group of settlements where people from another country have made their homes. However, the people are still subject to the laws of their original homeland. During the next century, English colonies were created up and down the eastern shore of what is now the United States.

The English weren't the first Europeans to explore North America, nor were they the first people to make their homes there. But these 13 Colonies served as the foundation for the United States of America.

The land used for the Maryland Colony was originally part of Virginia.

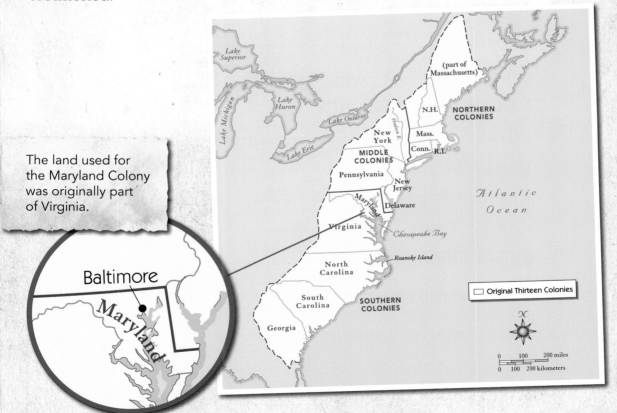

In 1497 John Cabot explored the eastern coast of present-day Canada. However, he thought he'd reached northeastern Asia.

European Explorers in the Americas

After Christopher Columbus reached the Americas in 1492, other European explorers rushed to claim territory in the "New World." Adventurers from Portugal, England, France, Spain, and the Netherlands set sail across the Atlantic Ocean, hoping to find gold and other riches. In 1513 explorer Juan Ponce de León reached present-day Florida and claimed the land for Spain. In 1565 St. Augustine, Florida, became the first permanent European settlement in what is now the United States.

England Claims the East Coast

Explorer John Cabot reached the eastern coast of North America in 1497. Although he was Italian, Cabot was hired by England's King Henry VII to explore the New World. Therefore, Cabot claimed the land for England. However, he did not establish settlements on the land, so his claims were worth nothing. It wasn't until the late 1500s that English businessmen began making plans to **colonize** the region.

Early English Settlement

Virginia, the first permanent English colony in North America, was founded in 1607. John Smith and other men built a small settlement there called Jamestown. Other settlements soon followed. By 1733 the British had colonized the area from present-day Maine to Georgia. To the north of these colonies lay New France, the French-controlled region of what is now Canada. To the south, the Spanish claimed Florida.

Colonial Character

Each of the 13 Colonies had its own unique characteristics based on who first settled there and why. Some came for religious freedom. Others came to get rich off the land. But it wasn't easy to start a new life in a new land. During the long ocean voyage, the colonists faced hunger, disease, and even death. But they risked it all to create a better life for themselves and their families.

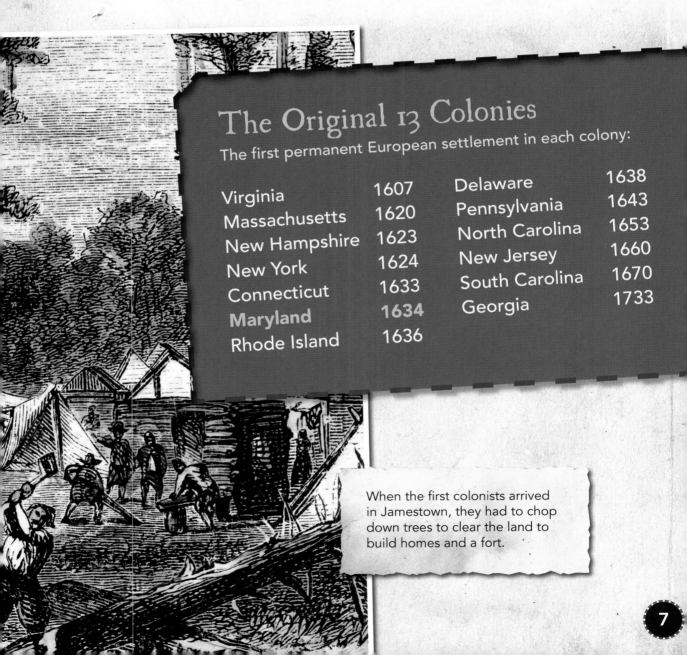

The Original 13 Colonies
The first permanent European settlement in each colony:

Virginia	1607	Delaware	1638
Massachusetts	1620	Pennsylvania	1643
New Hampshire	1623	North Carolina	1653
New York	1624	New Jersey	1660
Connecticut	1633	South Carolina	1670
Maryland	1634	Georgia	1733
Rhode Island	1636		

When the first colonists arrived in Jamestown, they had to chop down trees to clear the land to build homes and a fort.

Chapter 1:
Maryland's First People

Thousands of years before European settlers arrived, the region now known as Maryland was home to several Native American tribes. On the eastern shore of the Chesapeake Bay, the Nanticokes and the Choptanks were the most powerful groups. The western side of the bay was home to the Piscataways and a number of other tribes.

The Susquehannock people lived along the Susquehanna River, to the north of Chesapeake Bay. This fierce group often raided the villages of other tribes. By 1675 European diseases and warfare with colonists and other tribes had almost entirely wiped out the Susquehannocks.

People of the Woodlands

The native people counted on the Chesapeake Bay for survival. It was home to hundreds of species of fish and shellfish, including bass, perch, eels, oysters, and crabs. In the early 1600s, John Smith said that there were so many fish in the bay's waters that he and his men tried to catch them with frying pans. In the thick woods surrounding the bay, men used bows, arrows, and spears to hunt deer, elk, turkey, and other game.

Native American women cooked the food and made clothing from animal skins and furs. They also grew corn, squash, and beans and gathered wild berries and other plants. Many of the tribes also grew tobacco. During Colonial times, tobacco was Maryland's most important crop.

This engraving from around 1585 shows how Native Americans used spears to catch fish.

Life in an Algonquian Village

Most of the tribes that lived on the shores of the Chesapeake Bay spoke Algonquian languages. They also shared similar beliefs, customs, and ways of life.

People within tribes lived together in villages. Each village had a chief who made the important decisions for his village. He decided who the group would trade with and who it would go to war against.

The tribes living near the Chesapeake Bay moved from place to place, depending upon the season. In the summer and fall, they lived in villages where they grew crops. When the weather turned cold, they traveled further inland to winter hunting camps. In the springtime, the tribes moved to fishing camps on the shores of the bay.

In the early 1600s, there were 8,000–10,000 Native Americans living in Maryland. But that number was greatly reduced after the arrival of European settlers who brought diseases, such as **smallpox**. Other native people would move out of the area as colonists took over the land. However, **descendants** of some of the Chesapeake Bay's first people still live in Maryland today.

smallpox—a disease that spreads easily from person to person, causing chills, fever, and pimples that scar

descendants—a person's child and family members born after that child

John White was an English artist who came to North America in 1585. He created several maps and paintings of Virginia and the Chesapeake Bay region. This one depicts an Algonquian village.

Chapter 2:
New Arrivals

In June 1608 John Smith and several colonists traveled northeast from Jamestown and began exploring the Chesapeake Bay area. Smith was impressed by what he saw. He also created accurate maps of the bay. These maps, along with Smith's glowing descriptions, attracted more colonists to North America.

During this time Smith met some of the region's native people, including the Susquehannocks and Nanticokes. At first the Nanticokes were unfriendly, firing arrows at Smith's party. But later Smith began trading with the tribe.

Critical Thinking with Primary Sources

Captain John Smith's maps of the Chesapeake Bay region are quite accurate given the lack of technology when he made them 400 years ago. In what ways might historians use Smith's maps today? What instruments might a modern person use to map an uncharted region?

John Smith (1580–1631)

English adventurer John Smith was famous even before he sailed for America. As a young man, when the ship he was sailing on sank, a pirate ship picked him up and rescued him. While with them Smith became an "accidental" pirate.

Smith also fought in many battles. While fighting in Turkey, he was wounded and then was held as a slave. He later escaped and returned to England. On the trip from England to Virginia in 1607, Smith was accused of planning a **mutiny** and was nearly executed. In the new settlement, however, Smith quickly proved his worth.

The colonists' first few months in Jamestown were marked by hunger, disease, and attacks by unfriendly tribes. Smith led the Jamestown colonists in finding food and building stronger homes and protective fences. His leadership helped the Jamestown colony thrive. Without Smith, the colonists may not have survived the first winter in Jamestown.

"Heaven and earth never agreed better to frame a place for man's habitation."

—John Smith, describing Virginia, where he established the Jamestown settlement

A Colony for Catholics

The early 1600s marked the beginning of a **migration** from England to America. Many of the earliest arrivals were searching for religious freedom.

During this time people in England viewed Catholics with suspicion and distrust. In 1629 George Calvert, also known as Lord Baltimore, asked King Charles I for a piece of land in America. Calvert was a Catholic, and he wanted to create a colony where Catholics could freely and safely practice their religion. He also hoped to make money from his new colony. Calvert believed that a spot in Virginia would be the perfect place for his settlement.

When colonists in Virginia learned what Calvert was up to, they were not happy. They quickly sent a representative to the king asking him to refuse Calvert's request.

George Calvert wanted to create a colony in America where people were free to practice whatever religion they chose. However, he died before the colony was settled.

A Proprietary Colony

Despite the complaints of the Virginia colonists, in June 1632 the king granted the Calvert family a **charter** for land near the Chesapeake Bay. George Calvert had recently died, so the grant was given to his son Cecil.

Under the charter the Calverts were made **proprietors**, or owners, of a new colony called Maryland. The family had the right to give away land, tax colonists, appoint officials, and make all the laws for the new colony.

migration—the act of moving from one place to another
charter—an official document granting permission to set up a new colony, organization, or company
proprietor—a person given ownership of a colony

14

Due to **erosion**, the Chesapeake Bay coastline that the first explorers and colonists saw was very different than it is today.

A Colony in the Middle

The land that became Maryland was originally part of the Virginia Colony. Both the Maryland and Virginia Colonies were located on the Chesapeake Bay, so they shared a common climate. They also developed similar ways of life. But relations between the residents of Maryland and Virginia were not always friendly. The Maryland Colony would also have disputes with another neighbor, Pennsylvania. For years Maryland and Pennsylvania argued over the exact location of their border.

erosion—the wearing away of land by water or wind

Early Settlers

In November 1633 two ships, the *Ark* and the *Dove*, set sail from London, England. Some of Maryland's first settlers, both Catholics and Protestants, were on board. Cecil Calvert had to stay in England, but he hoped that Maryland would be a place where all Christians could live together peacefully. He made his younger brother Leonard governor of the Maryland Colony.

After more than three months on the choppy seas of the Atlantic Ocean, the *Ark* and the *Dove* arrived in Virginia. Leonard Calvert quickly set out to meet the leaders of the Native American tribes in the area. He traded with the Yaocomaco people for a piece of land to start their new colony. Calvert named the settlement St. Mary's City.

Soon after arriving in America in 1634, Leonard Calvert let local Native American tribes know that his people came in peace.

In this painting, artist Emanuel Gottlieb Leutze shows the founding of the Maryland Colony with a Catholic priest offering a blessing.

St. Mary's City

Each of Maryland's first male settlers was given 100 acres of land. If he was married, he received 100 more acres for his wife and 50 acres for each of his children. In exchange the settlers had to pay a yearly fee to the Calverts. Some colonists paid the fee with wheat, corn, or tobacco.

Soon after they arrived, the settlers built a wall around St. Mary's City. Then they got to work building homes and planting crops, such as corn and tobacco.

Maryland's First Test

The Calverts soon faced the first challenge to their authority. In 1631 Virginia colonist William Claiborne had established a trading post and settlement on Kent Island in the Chesapeake Bay. Claiborne became furious three years later when he learned that the king had given the region to the Calverts. Suddenly he found himself living in Maryland!

In 1635 one of Claiborne's trading ships clashed with two ships from Maryland. After several of his men were killed, Claiborne surrendered. In April 1638, while Claiborne was in England, Maryland officials took control of Kent Island. But Maryland had not seen the last of William Claiborne.

Ships from Maryland battled with William Claiborne's ships in the spring of 1635.

Calverts vs. Colonists

Around the same time, the Calverts started having problems with their own colonists. The settlers in Maryland wanted the right to make their own laws. In February 1635 a Colonial **assembly** was organized in St. Mary's City to create a new set of laws.

However Cecil Calvert believed the king had given him the right to make the colony's laws. When Calvert read the Colonial assembly's laws, he refused to accept them. In turn he sent his own set of laws to the colonists in Maryland. The colonists quickly rejected Calvert's laws, and once again wrote their own. Finally, in 1639, Calvert accepted the new laws and the right of the colonists to create them.

Cecil Calvert was the Second Lord Baltimore.

William Claiborne (1600?–1677?)

William Claiborne was technically Maryland's first English settler. After arriving in Virginia in 1621, Claiborne established trade relations with the Susquehannocks. In 1626 Claiborne was named Virginia's secretary of state, which, at the time, was only one step below the governor in terms of power. However, in 1635, one of Claiborne's trading ships was involved in a battle with ships from Maryland. Soon after, Virginia's governor removed Claiborne from his post.

Did You Know?

Some historians consider the skirmish between Claiborne's and Maryland's ships on April 23, 1635, as the first naval battle in U.S. history.

Chapter 3:
Life in the New Colony

Maryland
★ USA ★

The 1640s were a time of trouble in both England and Maryland. The English Civil War began in 1642 and lasted for nine years. People who supported the Puritan **Parliament** fought those who supported King Charles. Cecil Calvert and most of Maryland's Catholics supported the **Anglican** king. Many of Maryland's Protestant colonists favored Parliament.

In February 1645 a Parliament supporter named Richard Ingle attacked and captured St. Mary's City. He ordered all Maryland colonists to swear an oath of loyalty to Parliament. Those who refused had their farms burned and their livestock killed.

Catholics: Catholics believe in the teachings of the Bible as they are interpreted by the Catholic Church. The pope is the leader of the Catholic Church.

Anglicans: In the 1500s Protestantism—a branch of Christianity—was formed to challenge the Catholic Church. Protestants believe that the teachings of the Bible should be interpreted by each individual. In 1534 King Henry VIII made Anglicanism, a form of Protestantism, the official Church of England. He also made himself the head of the Anglican Church.

Puritans: Puritanism began as an offshoot of the Anglican Church. However, Puritans believed that the Church of England was too similar to the Catholic Church. Puritans wanted to strip or "purify" their church of all similarities to Catholicism. Puritans also believed that each person and each congregation was responsible to God not to the King of England.

Leonard Calvert fled to Virginia for safety. Ingle's Rebellion finally ended in December 1646, when Leonard Calvert and a group of armed men stood up to Ingle and his rebels and restored order.

But fighting among Maryland's Puritans, Anglicans, and Catholics continued until November 1657, when Cecil Calvert negotiated a peace treaty. The treaty required that those living in Maryland accept people of all Christian faiths.

Margaret Brent (1601?–1671?)

When Leonard Calvert died in June 1647, he left colonist Margaret Brent in charge of his estate. He also put her in a difficult position. The soldiers Calvert had hired to restore order during Ingle's Rebellion threatened to riot unless they were paid immediately. In January 1648 Brent appeared before the Colonial assembly. She was hoping to join the assembly to ask them to pay the soldiers from Colonial funds. But when the men refused her request, Brent took matters into her own hands. She sold Cecil Calvert's cattle and some of Leonard Calvert's property to raise the money to pay the soldiers.

Parliament—Great Britain's lawmaking body

Anglican—relating to the Church of England, the official Protestant faith

Daily Life for Maryland Colonists

Many of Maryland's first colonists were **indentured servants**. Indentured servants agreed to work for a certain number of years for a master in the American Colonies. In exchange the master paid for the servant's trip to America and provided him or her with food and a place to live. Many of the people who came to the 13 Colonies this way were young, single men.

Life was not easy for Maryland's indentured servants. They were required to work long hours in the tobacco fields, and masters often beat servants who were lazy or disobedient. But indentured servants who served out their terms were given their freedom and some land.

Whether servant or master, Maryland's first colonists shared similar living conditions. The first homes in the colony were two-story, dirt-floor houses that were dark and cramped. Inside there was little furniture. A typical colonist might own a straw mattress, a rug, and a table and benches but little else.

During harvesttime everyone pitched in to pick the tobacco crop.

In the early days of the colony, men outnumbered women by about six to one. The women who did settle in Maryland worked side by side with their husbands in the tobacco fields. They also tended a garden, sewed, cooked, and took care of the children.

Critical Thinking with Primary Sources

For many people, a contract of indenture was a chance at a new life. In this particular contract, Richard Lowther has agreed to become a servant to Edward Hurd for four years. In exchange Lowther will receive passage to America, food, clothing, and a place to live. When his service is complete, he will receive 50 acres of land in Virginia. Why might some people have agreed to the terms of such a contract? Do you think such contracts exist today? Would you sign such a contract?

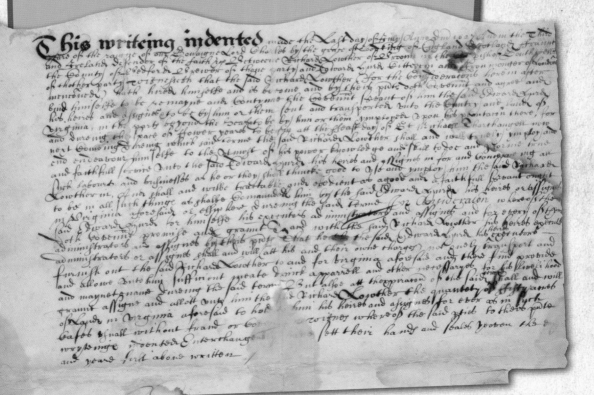

A Colonial Economy

From the start tobacco was the most important crop in Maryland's economy. The owners of large tobacco **plantations** were usually wealthy Catholics who had arrived in the first wave of settlement. They had claimed the best land, and they became rich off it. They also claimed the highest positions in the Colonial government.

In the early days, almost everyone grew tobacco to sell. The smaller planters sold their crops to larger plantation owners, who were better able to ship and sell the crops to England.

Tobacco greatly influenced the way the Maryland Colony grew. Large towns and cities were not common back then. Instead the big tobacco plantations became the centers of society. Some towns also sprang up around ports where goods were shipped out of the Chesapeake Bay.

Many farmers had to transport their tobacco crops to larger port cities.

Not everyone in Colonial times made a living as a farmer. Some worked as blacksmiths, making items out of iron, such as horseshoes.

From Tobacco to Grain

When the price of tobacco dropped in the late 1600s, Maryland's colonists had to find other ways to make a living. Many began growing wheat and other grains, which were sold in the American Colonies or exported to England. Others worked as carpenters, blacksmiths, and shoemakers.

Shipbuilding also became an important industry in Maryland. Timber from the **Piedmont** region was used to craft vessels that shipped goods across the ocean. Other trades sprang up around the shipping industry. Rope makers, sailmakers, and barrel builders all found work in Maryland.

plantation—a large farm where crops are grown

The Rise of Slavery

Despite the decrease of in prices, many Maryland colonists continued to farm tobacco. Tobacco farming was hard work. From early spring through late fall, workers were needed to tend the crops. At first indentured servants supplied the muscle. But by the late 1600s, fewer indentured servants were choosing to migrate to Maryland.

Faced with a lack of workers, plantation owners began using enslaved people from Africa to work in the tobacco fields. These people were kidnapped in Africa, sold to slave traders, and then sold to plantation owners. The slave traders brought more than 305,000 Africans to America between 1626 and 1860.

Maryland
★ USA ★

On slave ships hundreds of people were chained together. It was so crowded that they could barely move or breathe. Many died on the way to America.

Living in Slavery

Many of the slaves arriving from Africa were sent to the Chesapeake Bay area. By 1750 Maryland and Virginia had more slaves than any of the other American Colonies. Four out of every ten people living there were enslaved.

Slaves were forced to work long hours for no pay, and their living conditions were horrible. They survived on little food and rarely received medical attention when they were sick. Slaves were viewed as property, not human beings, and were often beaten by their masters.

Slaves had even fewer rights than indentured servants. Unlike indentured servants, slaves had little hope of ever becoming free. In 1664 Maryland's Colonial Assembly passed a law which stated that the children and grandchildren of slaves were also considered slaves. Throughout the Colonial period, Maryland passed many laws that further restricted the freedom of slaves.

In this painting, men, women, and children, who were kidnapped from Africa, waited to be sold as slaves after arriving in America.

Chapter 5:
A Growing Colony

The mid- to late 1600s were troublesome times in Maryland. In 1675 the colonists and the Susquehannocks in the region waged war against each other. Many native people and colonists were killed during these battles.

Tensions between Protestants and Catholics also flared up. In July 1689 Protestant John Coode led a rebellion against Maryland's Catholic leaders. During Coode's Rebellion, a mob of 700 armed Protestants marched on St. Mary's City and took control of the government. Without a single shot being fired, the Catholic Calverts were overthrown.

Native Americans sometimes attacked plantations without warning.

After the rebellion, Maryland became a **royal colony**. This meant that the king of England and Parliament were in charge of the colony. The Calvert family was allowed to keep its unsold lands, but they no longer had any say in governing the colony.

Maryland's current State House in Annapolis is the oldest state capitol building in the United States. It was built in 1772.

An End to Tolerance

Once the Protestants took control, they quickly put an end to religious **tolerance** in Maryland. Catholics, Quakers, and others who refused to sign an oath of loyalty to the king were banned from holding office or voting.

Did You Know?

In 1694 Governor Francis Nicholson moved Maryland's capital from St. Mary's City to Annapolis, which was more centrally located. By 1700 Maryland was a booming colony and Annapolis was a successful seaport. As the home of many wealthy shipbuilders, merchants, and planters, Annapolis had a thriving cultural scene.

royal colony—a colony controlled by a monarch or his or her representatives

tolerance—the acceptance of people's beliefs or actions that differ from one's

The Proprietors Return

When Charles Calvert died in 1715, his son Benedict Leonard Calvert asked King George I to return control of Maryland to the Calverts. Perhaps because Benedict had left the Catholic faith and converted to Protestantism, the king agreed. However when Benedict died two months later, his 15-year-old son Charles became Maryland's newest proprietor.

Benedict Calvert, the Fourth Lord Baltimore, died before control of the Maryland Colony was returned to his family.

The city of Baltimore was founded in 1729. Within a few years, it was a booming seaport for transporting tobacco and grain.

A New Port and the Piedmont

In 1729 the Carrolls, one of Maryland's important Catholic families, donated some land for a new settlement on the Patapsco River. This became the city of Baltimore, which was soon a central port for exporting tobacco. By 1775 Baltimore was one of the most important ports in all of the 13 Colonies.

As more colonists arrived in Maryland, land along the coast became scarce. New arrivals began settling in the colony's western frontier, known as the Piedmont. Some of the colonists came from other colonies, especially German-speaking settlers from nearby Pennsylvania. Scots-Irish immigrants came from Northern Ireland.

Frederick, the most important town in the Piedmont region, was founded in 1745. The town was a center for trade for the frontier. By 1850 it was one of Maryland's largest towns.

Golden Times

By the mid-1700s, Maryland's economy was booming. The export of tobacco, grain, iron, and other goods helped make the colony a success. Important ports and trading centers like Annapolis, Baltimore, and Frederick attracted more settlers. Some of the wealthiest people in the colony built large brick homes in Annapolis to be near the seat of the Colonial government.

Cultural and social life also thrived during this period. Maryland's wealthier colonists went to horse races and took part in foxhunts. They attended grand dances and the theater. In fact George Washington often attended plays in Annapolis. Many wealthy men of the colony joined men's clubs. One such organization, called the Tuesday Club, met to discuss every subject except politics.

Grand balls and dances were popular activities enjoyed by Maryland's richest colonists.

Settling an Old Feud

For years Maryland and Pennsylvania had argued over the exact boundary between the two colonies. In the 1730s, when a Maryland colonist named Thomas Cresap built a home in the disputed area, the conflict turned violent. He harassed his Pennsylvania neighbors and killed their livestock when they wandered into what he considered Maryland territory.

Finally, between 1763 and 1767, Charles Mason and Jeremiah Dixon were hired to map out the boundary between Maryland, Pennsylvania, and Delaware. This border is known as the Mason–Dixon Line.

Charles Mason and Jeremiah Dixon settled the border dispute involving Maryland, Pennsylvania, and Delaware. During the Civil War, the Mason–Dixon Line became the unofficial dividing line between the North and the South.

Did You Know?

During Colonial times England sent criminals to the Chesapeake Bay area. Depending on their crime, these convicts were sentenced to work for 7 to 14 years in the American Colonies before being freed. Many merchants and owners of smaller plantations used convicts because they cost less to buy than slaves. By 1776 approximately 21,000 convicts had been shipped to Maryland.

Chapter 6:
Fighting for Freedom

In the mid-1700s, Britain's Parliament began passing laws that angered colonists. In 1750 the Iron Act banned colonists from making finished products out of iron mined in Maryland. Instead the iron had to be shipped to England, finished there, and then brought back to the colonies for sale. Other laws passed in the coming years placed taxes on legal documents, newspapers, sugar, and tea.

Colonists protested the Stamp Act through public demonstrations and by boycotting the stamp. Notice the skull and crossbones on the lower right corner of the newspaper. That's where the stamp was supposed to go.

Outraged colonists quickly reacted to the laws. They **boycotted** taxed items and held public demonstrations to show their anger. Many colonists ignored the laws. The publisher of *The Maryland Gazette* printed his newspaper without the required stamp. Maryland colonists even burned a cargo ship carrying a load of tea. When the *Peggy Stewart* arrived in the port of Annapolis in October 1774, it was loaded with tea. This went against the boycott. An angry mob told ship owner Anthony Stewart to burn the vessel and its cargo, or they would do it for him.

This painting by artist Francis Blackwell Mayer shows a group of angry colonists about to set fire to the *Peggy Stewart*.

boycott—to refuse to buy or use a product or service to protest something believed to be wrong or unfair

In April 1774 Parliament passed a series of laws that the Americans referred to as the Intolerable Acts. One of the laws required colonists to let British soldiers stay in their homes. As punishment for the Boston Tea Party, other laws closed down Boston Harbor and put a British military governor in charge of Massachusetts. Although the Intolerable Acts mainly targeted Massachusetts, people in the other colonies worried that the British would punish them in the same way.

In June 1774 a new Maryland Assembly met for the first time. It elected representatives to attend the First Continental Congress, which met in Philadelphia, Pennsylvania, in September and October 1774. The goal of the Continental Congress was to decide how to get Great Britain to **repeal** the Intolerable Acts. They decided to boycott all British goods beginning December 1, 1774.

Charles Carroll (1737–1832)

Like his father, Charles Carroll was a wealthy Maryland planter. But in the early 1770s, Catholics could not hold elected office or even vote. However after writing a series of articles for *The Maryland Gazette*, Carroll was thrust into the public eye and politics. His election to Maryland's Second Convention in November 1774 put an end to the ban on Catholics in Maryland politics. As a fierce supporter of independence, Carroll was the only Catholic signer of the Declaration of Independence.

Critical Thinking with Primary Sources

For several months in 1773, Charles Carroll and Daniel Dulany faced off against each other in a series of articles published in *The Maryland Gazette.* Carroll argued against fees and taxes imposed on the colonists without representation in Parliament. He also supported a government elected by the people. Although Carroll called himself "First Citizen" in the articles, his true identity quickly became known. Why do you think Carroll wouldn't sign his name? How do you think writing these articles helped his political career? Do you think that newspapers should publish **anonymous** articles?

"…[I]t has I hope, been proved already, that fees are taxes, and that the settlement of them by proclamation is … illegal … [L]et us consider whether the proclamation be a … dangerous attack on liberty."

Joining the Cause

Over the next few years, relations between the 13 Colonies and Great Britain continued to fall apart. The tension came to a head on April 19, 1775, when American **Patriots** and British soldiers battled at Lexington and Concord in Massachusetts. The Revolutionary War had begun.

In July 1775 Maryland officials declared an end to proprietary rule. A year later four representatives from Maryland signed the Declaration of Independence. In November 1776 Maryland adopted its first constitution. It guaranteed religious freedom and gave Catholics and free black men who owned property the right to vote.

repeal—to officially cancel something, such as a law
anonymous—written by a person whose name is not known
Patriot—one who sided with the colonies during the Revolutionary War

Maryland Patriots quickly began signing up to serve in George Washington's Continental army. But not everyone in Maryland wanted to break free of Great Britain. Those who supported the king, known as **Loyalists**, were often driven out of the colony.

The Maryland 400

At the beginning of the Revolutionary War, the British thought they could quickly put an end to the American rebellion. They felt that the newly formed Continental army and ragtag Colonial **militias** were no match for the well-trained British military. The British greatly underestimated the bravery and determination of the Patriots.

Mary Katherine Goddard
(1738–1816)

In January 1777 Baltimore printer Mary Katherine Goddard published the first fully signed copy of the Declaration of Independence. Goddard learned the print trade in Rhode Island from her brother William. In February 1774 Mary Katherine moved to Baltimore to edit and publish *The Maryland Journal*, the newspaper her brother had started there. She also published several **almanacs** during her time in Maryland. Some historians believe Goddard was also the first female postmaster in the United States. She served in that position in Baltimore from 1775 to 1789.

No major battles took place in Maryland, but 400 members of the 1st Maryland Regiment earned George Washington's respect for bravery and reliability. At the Battle of Long Island in New York on August 27, 1776, Washington's troops were greatly outnumbered. Many of Washington's men dropped their weapons and ran off the battlefield fearing for their lives. But a group of men known as the Maryland 400 was the last to retreat. While shielding other Colonial regiments who fled to safety, the Maryland 400 suffered heavy losses. Nearly 260 of the Maryland 400 died and more than 100 were captured.

The Continental army retreated after losing to the British at the Battle of Long Island.

"*Good God, what brave fellows I must this day lose!*"
—George Washington watching the Battle of Long Island

Baltimore Plays an Important Role

Baltimore grew in importance during the Revolutionary War. The town's sheltered port made it the perfect supply center for the Continental army. Factories there made clothes and tools for the troops. The Continental Congress even met in Baltimore for a short time.

During the war a number of ships were built in Baltimore for the Continental navy. Some were used as **privateers**, which were permitted by the government to attack and capture enemy vessels. During the war Baltimore privateers captured hundreds of British ships.

Statehood

At the end of the Revolutionary War, it was Annapolis' turn in the spotlight. There on January 14, 1784, the Continental Congress **ratified** the Treaty of Paris, which ended the war. Annapolis also served as the temporary capital of the new United States for six months.

Maryland became the seventh state when it ratified the U.S. Constitution on April 28, 1788. Maryland and Virginia each donated a portion of land to be used as the nation's new capital, Washington, D.C., which was founded in 1790. Virginia's portion was later returned, so all of Washington, D.C., is former Maryland territory.

In the years to come, Maryland would continue to play an important role in the nation's history. During the Civil War, the Battle of Antietam took place near Sharpsburg, Maryland, on September 17, 1862. It was the bloodiest single-day battle of the war. More than 3,600 soldiers died and more than 17,000 were wounded.

In this painting of Washington, D.C., the artist used his placement of the White House (left center) and the U.S. Capitol (right center) to symbolize the balance of power between the executive and legislative branches of government.

After the Civil War, Maryland's seaport location and its good
railroad connections helped businesses boom and cities grow.
In the decades that followed, the state's location near the nation's
capital assured its continued growth.

Timeline

1607 John Smith helps found Jamestown, Virginia, the first permanent English settlement in what is now the United States.

1608 John Smith explores and maps the Chesapeake Bay area.

1629 George Calvert, the first Lord Baltimore, asks England's King Charles I for a piece of land in America.

1631 Virginia colonist William Claiborne starts a trading post and settlement on Kent Island in the Chesapeake Bay.

1632 In June the king grants the Calvert family a charter for land around the Chesapeake Bay.

1633 In November two ships carrying colonists set sail for Maryland from England.

1634 In March colonists arrive at St. Clement's Island, Maryland.

1635 Maryland's Colonial Assembly meets for the first time.

1638 Maryland takes control of Kent Island from William Claiborne.

1644 Ingle's Rebellion begins.

1646 Ingle's Rebellion ends, and the Calvert family regains control of the Maryland Colony.

1675 Maryland and Virginia go to war with the Susquehannocks.

1689 In July Puritans led by John Coode stage a rebellion against Maryland's Catholic leaders and the proprietary government.

1692 Maryland becomes a royal colony.

1715 Maryland becomes a proprietary colony once again, and the Calvert family regains control.

1718 England begins sending convicts to the Chesapeake Bay area.

1727 Maryland's first newspaper, *The Maryland Gazette*, begins publication.

1729 Baltimore is founded.

1733 Great Britain passes the Molasses Act, the first of several taxes that anger colonists.

1750 The Iron Act bans colonists from making finished products out of iron mined in Maryland.

1763 Charles Mason and Jeremiah Dixon begin mapping out the boundary between Maryland, Delaware, and Pennsylvania.

1775 In April war breaks out between Great Britain and the American Colonies.

1776 In July delegates from the 13 Colonies sign the Declaration of Independence. In August Maryland drafts its first constitution.

1784 On January 14 the Treaty of Paris is ratified in Annapolis.

1788 On April 28 Maryland becomes the seventh state. In December Maryland donates land to be used as Washington, D.C., the new national capital.

Glossary

almanac (AWL-muh-nak)—a yearly magazine or book that contains facts

Anglican (AN-gli-kuhn)—relating to the Church of England, the official Protestant faith of England

anonymous (uh-NON-uh-muhss)—written by a person whose name is not known

assembly (uh-SEM-blee)—a group of people elected to create laws

boycott (BOY-kot)—to refuse to buy or use a product or service to protest something believed to be wrong or unfair

charter (CHAR-tuhr)—an official document granting permission to set up a new colony, organization, or company

colonize (KAH-luh-nize)—to establish a new colony

colony (KAH-luh-nee)—a place that is settled by people from another country and is controlled by that country

descendants (di-SEN-duhnts)—a person's child and family members born after that child

erosion (i-ROH-zhuhn)—the wearing away of land by water or wind

indentured servant (in-DEN-churd SERV-uhnt)—a person who worked for someone else for a period of time in return for living expenses and travel costs to the colonies

Loyalist (LOI-uh-list)—a colonist who was loyal to Great Britain during the Revolutionary War

migration (mye-GRAY-shuhn)—the act of moving from one place to another

militia (muh-LISH-uh)—a group of volunteer citizens who are organized to fight but are not professional soldiers

mutiny (MYOOT-uh-nee)—a revolt against the captain of a ship

Parliament (PAR-luh-muhnt)—Great Britain's lawmaking body

Patriot (PAY-tree-uht)—one who sided with the colonies during the Revolutionary War

Piedmont (PEED-mont)—a hilly, rocky area of central Maryland

plantation (plan-TAY-shuhn)—a large farm where crops are grown

privateer (prye-vuh-TEER)—a private ship that is authorized to attack enemy ships during wartime

proprietor (proh-PREYE-uh-ter)—a person given ownership of a colony

ratify (RAT-uh-fye)—to formally approve a document

repeal (ri-PEEL)—to officially cancel something, such as a law

royal colony (ROI-uhl KAH-luh-nee)—a colony controlled by a monarch or his or her representatives

smallpox (SMAWL-poks)—a disease that spreads easily from person to person, causing chills, fever, and pimples that scar

tolerance (TOL-ur-uhnss)—the acceptance of people's beliefs or actions that differ from one's own beliefs or actions

Critical Thinking Using the Common Core

1. Why did the Calverts want to create their own colony in North America? (Key Ideas and Details)

2. Use the infographic on page 20 to compare and contrast the beliefs of Catholics, Anglicans, and Puritans. (Craft and Structure)

3. Why did merchants and plantation owners use convicts as workers? Do you think it was a good idea? Why or why not? (Integration of Knowledge and Ideas)

Read More

Jobes, Cecily. *The Colony of Maryland*. Spotlight on the 13 Colonies. New York: PowerKids Press, 2016.

Morley, Jacqueline. *You Wouldn't Want to Be an American Colonist!* New York: Franklin Watts, 2013.

Pratt, Mary K. *A Timeline History of the Thirteen Colonies*. Timeline Trackers: America's Beginnings. Minneapolis: Lerner Publications, 2014.

Walker, Sally M. *Boundaries: How the Mason-Dixon Line Settled a Family Feud and Divided a Nation*. Somerville, Mass.: Candlewick Press, 2014.

Internet Sites

FactHound offers a safe, fun way to find Internet sites related to this book. All of the sites on FactHound have been researched by our staff.
Here's all you do:
Visit *www.facthound.com*
Type in this code: 9781515722380

 **Super-cool stuff!** Check out projects, games and lots more at **www.capstonekids.com**

Source Notes

Page 13, callout quote: John Smith. *Travels and Works of Captain John Smith, Part 1*. Edinburgh, Scotland: John Grant, 1910, p. 48.

Page 23, primary source box: "First Hand Accounts," *Virtual Jamestown*. Accessed April 2, 2016. http://www.virtualjamestown.org/exist/cocoon/jamestown/fha/J1046.

Page 37, primary source box: Derrick Lapp and Nancy Bramucci Sheads, "First Citizen: Charles Carroll of Carrollton," *Maryland State Archives: Teaching American History in Maryland*. Accessed April 2, 2016. http://msa.maryland.gov/megafile/msa/speccol/sc4800/sc4872/001282/html/m1282-0344.html.

Page 39, callout quote: Philander D. Chase, ed. *The Papers of George Washington, Revolutionary War Series*, vol. 6, 13 August 1776–20 October 1776. Charlottesville: University Press of Virginia, 1994, pp. 159–162.

Regions of the 13 Colonies		
Northern Colonies	**Middle Colonies**	**Southern Colonies**
Connecticut, Massachusetts, New Hampshire, Rhode Island	Delaware, New Jersey, New York, Pennsylvania	Georgia, Maryland, North Carolina, South Carolina, Virginia
land more suitable for hunting than farming; trees cut down for lumber; trapped wild animals for their meat and fur; fished in rivers, lakes, and ocean	the "Breadbasket" colonies—rich farmland, perfect for growing wheat, corn, rye, and other grains	soil better for growing tobacco, rice, and indigo; crops grown on huge farms called plantations; landowners depended heavily on servants and slaves to work in the fields

Select Bibliography

Carr, Lois Green, Philip D. Morgan, and Jean B. Russo, eds. *Colonial Chesapeake Society*. Chapel Hill, N.C.: The University of North Carolina Press, 1988.

Carson, Cary, Ronal d Hoffman, and Peter J. Albert, eds. *Of Consuming Interest: The Style of Life in the Eighteenth Century*. Charlottesville, Va.: University of Virginia Press, 1994.

Earle, Alice Morse. *Home Life in Colonial Days*. Stockbridge, Mass.: Berkshire Traveller Press, 1974.

Hawke, David. *The Colonial Experience*. Indianapolis, Ind.: The Bobbs-Merrill Company, Inc., 1966.

Land, Aubrey C. *Colonial Maryland: A History*. Millwood, N.Y.: KTO Press, 1981.

Langdon, William Chauncy. *Everyday Things in American Life, 1607–1776*. New York: Charles Scribner's Sons, 1937.

Main, Gloria L. *Tobacco Colony: Life in Early Maryland, 1650–1720*. Princeton, N.J.: Princeton University Press, 1982.

Middleton, Richard. *Colonial America: A History, 1565–1776*. Malden, Mass.: Blackwell Publishers, 1996.

Taylor, Alan. *American Colonies*. New York: Viking, 2001.

Wright, Louis B. *Everyday Life in Colonial America*. New York: Putnam, 1965.

Index

Maryland
★ USA ★